Collins

Easy Learning

Multiplication and division practice

Age 7-9

My name is _____.

I am _____ years old.

I go to _____ School.

Peter Clarke

How to use this book

- Find a quiet, comfortable place to work, away from other distractions.

- Ask your child what multiplication and division topic they are doing at school, and choose an appropriate topic.

- Tackle one topic at a time.

- Help with reading the instructions where necessary, and ensure that your child understands what they are required to do.

- Help and encourage your child to check their own answers as they complete each activity.

- Discuss with your child what they have learnt.

- Let your child return to their favourite pages once they have been completed, to play the games and talk about the activities.

- Reward your child with plenty of praise and encouragement.

Special features

- Yellow boxes: Introduce and outline the key multiplication and division ideas.

- Example boxes: Show how to do the activity.

- Yellow shaded boxes: Offer advice to parents on how to consolidate your child's understanding.

- Games: Some of the topics include a game, which reinforces the multiplication or division topic. Some of these games require a spinner. This is easily made using a pencil, a paperclip and the circle printed on each games page. Gently flick the paperclip with your finger to make it spin.

Published by Collins
An imprint of HarperCollins*Publishers*
77–85 Fulham Palace Road
Hammersmith
London
W6 8JB

Browse the complete Collins catalogue at www.collins.co.uk

© HarperCollins*Publishers* 2011

10 9 8 7 6 5 4 3 2

ISBN-13 978-0-00-746167-7

The author asserts his moral right to be identified as the author of this work.

British Library Cataloguing in Publication Data

A Catalogue record for this publication is available from the British Library

The author wishes to thank Brian Molyneaux for his valuable contribution to this publication.

Written by Peter Clarke
Page layout by Linda Miles, Lodestone Publishing Ltd
Illustrated by Katy Dynes and Graham Smith
Cover design by Linda Miles, Lodestone Publishing Ltd
Cover illustration by Kathy Baxendale
Project managed by Chantal Peacock
Commissioned by Tammy Poggo. Printed in China

Contents

2, 5 and 10 times tables

Q1 Draw lines matching the times table fact to the answer.

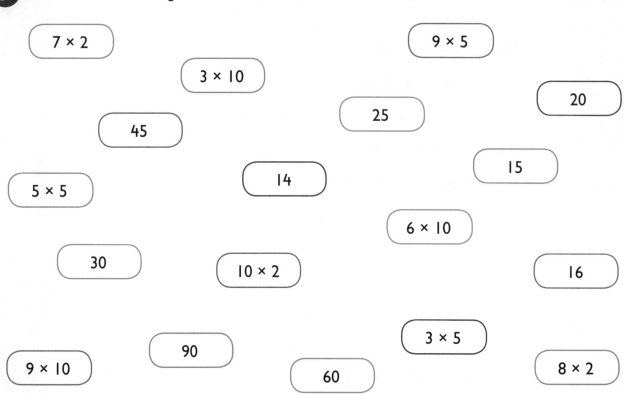

7 × 2

3 × 10

9 × 5

20

45

25

5 × 5

14

15

30

10 × 2

6 × 10

16

9 × 10

90

3 × 5

60

8 × 2

Q2 Complete the multiplication rings.

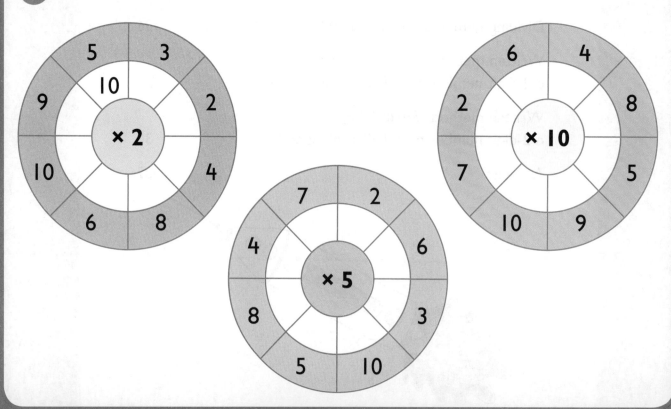

× 2 ring: 5, 3, 10, 9, 2, 10, 4, 6, 8

× 10 ring: 6, 4, 2, 8, 7, 5, 10, 9

× 5 ring: 7, 2, 4, 6, 8, 3, 5, 10

Game: Multiplication cards

You need: playing cards with the Jacks, Queens and Kings removed and 20 counters

- Before you start:
  - decide if you want to practice the 2, 5 or 10 times table
  - shuffle the cards and place them face down in a pile in the middle of the table.

- Take turns to turn over the top card from the pile.

- Both players multiply this number by the times table you are practicing.

- The first player to call out the correct answer wins that round a takes a counter.

- Continue to take turns to pick up a card from the pile and each player calculate the times table fact.

- When all the cards have been used, the winner is the player with more counters.

4 times 5 equals 20

Q3 Complete the table.

×	5	2	8	6	1	10	4	9	7	3
2								18		
5			40							
10										

It is important that your child knows by heart the 2, 5 and 10 times tables, and how multiplication facts can help with working out related division facts, e.g. 3 × 10 = 30 and 10 × 3 = 30, so 30 ÷ 3 = 10 and 30 ÷ 10 = 3. Counting on and back in steps of 2, 5 and 10 also helps your child to remember the multiples of 2, 5 and 10.

Division facts related to the 2, 5 and 10 times tables

Q1 Draw lines matching the division fact to the answer.

| 18 ÷ 2 | | 7 | | 6 |

| | 5 | | 8 | | 40 ÷ 5 |

| | | 30 ÷ 5 | | 70 ÷ 10 |

| 9 | | | 4 | | 20 ÷ 2 |

| 25 ÷ 5 | | 10 | | 40 ÷ 10 |

| | | 6 ÷ 2 |

| 20 ÷ 10 | | 2 | | 3 |

Q2 Complete the division rings.

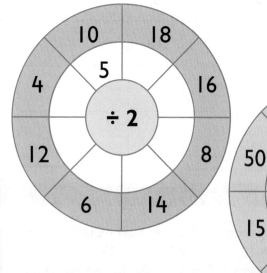

6

Game: 2, 5 and 10 division

- Before you start choose who will have which colour counters.

- Take turns to place one of your counters on a number on the board. Make sure not to cover up the number.

- Keep going until you have placed all your 10 counters on the board. Only one counter can go on each number.

- Now take turns to spin the spinner. If one of your counters is on a number that is divisible by the spinner number, remove that counter. If not, miss a turn.

- The winner is the first player to collect all of their 10 counters.

You need: pencil, paperclip and 20 counters: 10 of one colour, 10 of another colour

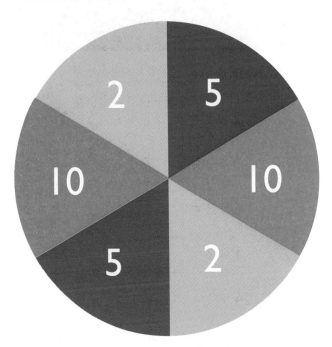

15	45	60	70	40	20
12	40	16	50	10	90
30	2	10	18	50	10
30	5	25	35	8	100
6	20	80	4	20	14

Q3 Colour all the multiples of 2. Circle all the multiples of 5.
Draw a cross through all the multiples of 10.

45	4	80	20	12	8	30	40

35	2	15	90	16	70	25

14	60	5	6	100	50	18	10

Q1 Answer these.

2 × 3 = ☐	21 ÷ 3 = ☐	6 × 3 = ☐
9 ÷ 3 = ☐	8 × 3 = ☐	30 ÷ 3 = ☐
6 ÷ 3 = ☐	3 × 3 = ☐	12 ÷ 3 = ☐
1 × 3 = ☐	27 ÷ 3 = ☐	5 × 3 = ☐
24 ÷ 3 = ☐	7 × 3 = ☐	3 ÷ 3 = ☐
4 × 3 = ☐	9 × 3 = ☐	10 × 3 = ☐

Q2 Write the numbers that come out of the machines.

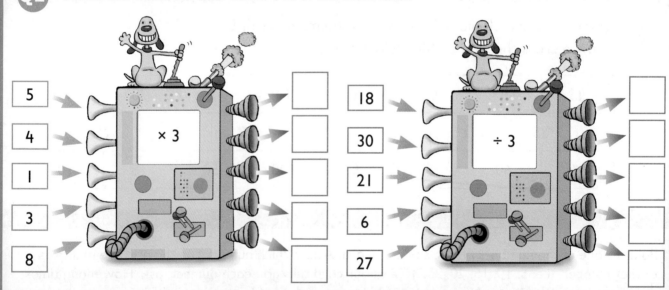

Game: Multiplying and dividing by 3

You need: pencil, paperclip and 20 counters: 10 of one colour, 10 of another colour

- Before you start, decide who will have which colour counters.

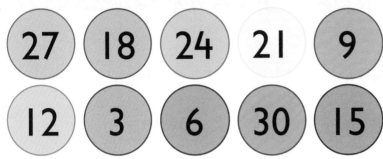

Game: Multiplying by 3

- Take turns to:
  - spin the spinner, e.g. 6
  - multiply the number by 3
  - place one of your counters on the circle, i.e. 18
  - say the multiplication calculation, i.e. '6 times 3 equals 18'.

Game: Dividing by 3

- Take turns to:
  - spin the spinner, e.g. 8
  - place one of your counters on the circle whose number, when divided by 3, equals the spinner number, i.e. 24
  - say the division calculation, i.e. '24 divided by 3 equals 8'.

- If the circle already has a counter on it, miss a turn.
- Continue until all the circles have a counter on them.
- The winner is the player with more of their counters on the circles.

Q3 Write the missing numbers.

$\square \times 3 = 18$ $\square \div 3 = 2$ $\square \times 3 = 3$

$\square \div 3 = 7$ $\square \times 3 = 6$ $\square \div 3 = 5$

$\square \times 3 = 27$ $\square \div 3 = 4$ $\square \times 3 = 12$

$\square \times 3 = 24$ $\square \times 3 = 21$ $\square \div 3 = 3$

$\square \div 3 = 6$ $\square \div 3 = 9$ $\square \div 3 = 8$

Take turns to spin the spinner, e.g. 8. Both players multiply the number by 3. The first player to call out the correct answer, i.e. 24, wins that round and collects a counter. Play 20 rounds. Who wins more counters?

4 times table and the related division facts

Q1 Answer these.

5 × 4 = ☐	8 ÷ 4 = ☐	7 × 4 = ☐
12 ÷ 4 = ☐	8 × 4 = ☐	32 ÷ 4 = ☐
20 ÷ 4 = ☐	6 × 4 = ☐	16 ÷ 4 = ☐
2 × 4 = ☐	40 ÷ 4 = ☐	4 × 4 = ☐
36 ÷ 4 = ☐	24 ÷ 4 = ☐	28 ÷ 4 = ☐
3 × 4 = ☐	10 × 4 = ☐	9 × 4 = ☐

Q2 Multiply each number on a red light by 4.
Divide each number on an orange light by 4. Write the answers on the green lights.

Game: Multiplying and dividing by 4

You need: two 1–6 dice and some counters

Player 1				
28	24	12	48	8
16	8	36	24	44
36	32	40	32	16
12	20	28	44	20
32	48	24	28	40

Player 2				
8	20	16	24	12
24	36	28	40	32
32	44	40	20	48
48	12	16	28	8
32	28	24	36	44

Game: Multiplying by 4

- Before you start, decide who is Player 1 and who is Player 2.

- Take turns to:
  - roll the dice
  - add the numbers together, i.e. 6 + 3 = 9
  - multiply the answer by 4, i.e. 9 x 4 = 36
  - place a counter on that number on your grid.

- If the number is already covered, miss a turn.

- The winner is the first player to make a line of 4 counters on their grid. The line can be along a row or a column or a diagonal.

Game: Dividing by 4

- Before you start, decide who is Player 1 and who is Player 2.

- Take turns to:
  - roll the dice
  - find a number on your grid that, when divided by 4, gives an answer that is either the two dice numbers or the sum of the two dice numbers
  - place a counter on that number.

- The winner is the first player to make a line of 4 counters on their grid. The line can be along a row or a column or a diagonal.

Q3 Write the missing numbers.

$\boxed{} \times 4 = 12$ 　　　 $\boxed{} \div 4 = 4$ 　　　 $\boxed{} \times 4 = 20$

$\boxed{} \div 4 = 8$ 　　　 $\boxed{} \times 4 = 8$ 　　　 $\boxed{} \times 4 = 36$

$\boxed{} \times 4 = 24$ 　　　 $\boxed{} \div 4 = 2$ 　　　 $\boxed{} \div 4 = 9$

$\boxed{} \div 4 = 6$ 　　　 $\boxed{} \times 4 = 16$ 　　　 $\boxed{} \times 4 = 32$

$\boxed{} \div 4 = 7$ 　　　 $\boxed{} \times 4 = 28$ 　　　 $\boxed{} \div 4 = 5$

Point to one of the numbers on the grids, e.g. 40, and ask your child to divide this number by 4, i.e. 'What is 40 divided by 4?'.

Q1 Answer these.

7 × 6 = ☐   24 ÷ 6 = ☐   5 × 6 = ☐

18 ÷ 6 = ☐   9 × 6 = ☐   42 ÷ 6 = ☐

36 ÷ 6 = ☐   4 × 6 = ☐   54 ÷ 6 = ☐

10 × 6 = ☐   12 ÷ 6 = ☐   6 × 6 = ☐

30 ÷ 6 = ☐   2 × 6 = ☐   48 ÷ 6 = ☐

3 × 6 = ☐   60 ÷ 6 = ☐   8 × 6 = ☐

Q2 Write the missing numbers.

☐ × 6 = 12   ☐ ÷ 6 = 4   6 × ☐ = 36

☐ ÷ 6 = 8   ☐ × 6 = 18   ☐ × 6 = 54

60 ÷ ☐ = 10   10 × ☐ = 60   ☐ ÷ 6 = 3

☐ × 6 = 42   ☐ ÷ 6 = 2   ☐ × 6 = 24

☐ ÷ 6 = 6   ☐ × 6 = 30   ☐ ÷ 6 = 5

☐ ÷ 6 = 7   54 ÷ ☐ = 9   ☐ × 6 = 48

Game: Multiplying and dividing by 6

Game: Multiplying by 6

You need: pencil, paper and playing cards with the Jacks, Queens and Kings removed

- Shuffle the cards and place them face down in a pile.
- Decide who is Player 1 and who is Player 2.
- Take turns to:
  - turn over the top card
  - multiply the card number by 6
  - write down the answer.
- After 8 rounds, each player adds their 8 scores (you can use a calculator).
- The winner is the player with the larger total.

Round	Player 1	Player 2
1		
2		
3		
4		
5		
6		
7		
8		

Game: Dividing by 6

You need: counters and playing cards with the Jacks, Queens and Kings removed

- Shuffle the cards and place them face down in a pile.
- Take turns to:
  - turn over the top card
  - place a counter on a square whose calculation gives the answer on the card.
- The winner is the first player to complete a line of 3 counters. The line can be along a row or a column or a diagonal.

36 ÷ 6	54 ÷ 6	42 ÷ 6	18 ÷ 6
12 ÷ 6	6 ÷ 6	48 ÷ 6	30 ÷ 6
6 ÷ 6	60 ÷ 6	24 ÷ 6	54 ÷ 6
18 ÷ 6	30 ÷ 6	42 ÷ 6	36 ÷ 6
48 ÷ 6	24 ÷ 6	60 ÷ 6	12 ÷ 6

Q3 Colour the multiples of 6. Then draw lines to match each multiple and times table fact.

(9 × 6)   (7 × 6)   (5 × 6)   (4 × 6)   (6 × 6)

42	3	18	16	32	24	40	54	6	20	26	30	52	48	56	12	65	60	36	10

(1 × 6)   (8 × 6)   (3 × 6)   (10 × 6)   (2 × 6)

Shuffle the playing cards with the Jacks, Queens and Kings removed, and place them face down in a pile. Take turns to turn over the top card. Both players multiply the number by 6. The first player to call out the correct answer wins that round and takes the card. Play 20 rounds.

Q1 Answer these.

3 × 7 = ☐	21 ÷ 7 = ☐	5 × 7 = ☐
14 ÷ 7 = ☐	4 × 7 = ☐	56 ÷ 7 = ☐
35 ÷ 7 = ☐	10 × 7 = ☐	63 ÷ 7 = ☐
8 × 7 = ☐	49 ÷ 7 = ☐	6 × 7 = ☐
28 ÷ 7 = ☐	2 × 7 = ☐	70 ÷ 7 = ☐
7 × 7 = ☐	42 ÷ 7 = ☐	9 × 7 = ☐

Q2 Multiply the numbers hit by 7. Write the answer in the same coloured box.

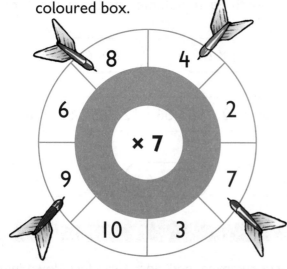

× 7

8   4   6   2   9   7   10   3

☐ ☐ ☐ ☐

Divide the numbers hit by 7. Write the answer in the same coloured box.

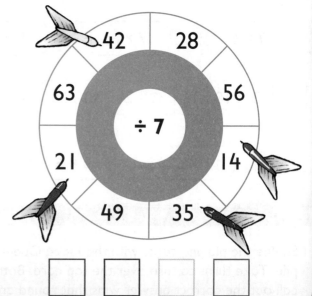

÷ 7

42   28   63   56   21   14   49   35

☐ ☐ ☐ ☐

You need: pencil, paperclip and 20 counters:
10 of one colour, 10 of another colour

- Before you start, decide who will have which colour counters.

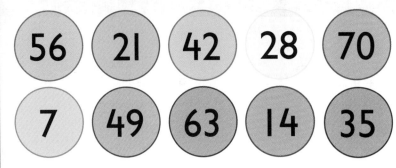

Game: Multiplying by 7

- Take turns to:
  - spin the spinner, e.g. 5
  - multiply the number by 7
  - place one of your counters on the circle, i.e. 35
  - say the multiplication calculation, i.e. '5 times 7 equals 35'.

Game: Dividing by 7

- Take turns to:
  - spin the spinner, e.g. 2
  - place one of your counters on the circle whose number, when divided by 7, equals the spinner number, i.e. 14
  - say the division calculation, i.e. '14 divided by 7 equals 2'.

- If the circle already has a counter on it, miss a turn.
- Continue until all the circles have a counter on them.
- The winner is the player with more of their counters on the circles.

Q3 Write the missing numbers.

$\boxed{} \times 7 = 35$ $\boxed{} \div 7 = 2$ $\boxed{} \times 7 = 70$

$\boxed{} \div 7 = 7$ $\boxed{} \times 7 = 49$ $\boxed{} \div 7 = 4$

$\boxed{} \times 7 = 42$ $\boxed{} \div 7 = 9$ $\boxed{} \times 7 = 56$

$\boxed{} \div 7 = 3$ $\boxed{} \times 7 = 21$ $\boxed{} \div 7 = 5$

$\boxed{} \div 7 = 6$ $\boxed{} \div 7 = 8$ $\boxed{} \times 7 = 28$

Take turns to spin the spinner, e.g. 6. Both players multiply the number by 7. The first player to call out the correct answer, i.e. 42, wins that round and collects a counter. Play 20 rounds. Who wins more counters?

8 times table and the related division facts

Q1 Answer these.

3 × 8 = ☐   24 ÷ 8 = ☐   9 × 8 = ☐

80 ÷ 8 = ☐   6 × 8 = ☐   16 ÷ 8 = ☐

64 ÷ 8 = ☐   10 × 8 = ☐   72 ÷ 8 = ☐

5 × 8 = ☐   32 ÷ 8 = ☐   2 × 8 = ☐

40 ÷ 8 = ☐   56 ÷ 8 = ☐   48 ÷ 8 = ☐

7 × 8 = ☐   8 × 8 = ☐   4 × 8 = ☐

Q2 Write the missing numbers.

☐ × 8 = 48   ☐ ÷ 8 = 8   8 × ☐ = 32

☐ ÷ 8 = 2   ☐ × 8 = 24   ☐ × 8 = 16

80 ÷ ☐ = 8   ☐ × 8 = 72   ☐ ÷ 8 = 7

☐ × 8 = 64   ☐ ÷ 8 = 3   ☐ × 8 = 56

☐ ÷ 8 = 5   ☐ × 8 = 40   ☐ ÷ 8 = 6

☐ ÷ 8 = 9   32 ÷ ☐ = 4   10 × ☐ = 80

Game: Multiplying and dividing by 8

You need: two 1–6 dice and some counters

Player 1				
24	80	48	88	16
56	48	72	32	64
40	64	40	56	24
88	32	16	40	64
72	48	80	56	96

Player 2				
24	96	40	88	64
64	32	56	16	72
48	80	48	56	24
40	16	72	40	64
56	88	32	48	80

Game: Multiplying by 8

- Before you start, decide who is Player 1 and who is Player 2.
- Take turns to:
  - roll the dice
  - add the numbers together, i.e. 2 + 5 = 7
  - multiply the answer by 8, i.e. 7 x 8 = 56
  - place a counter on that number on your grid.

- If the number is already covered, miss a turn.
- The winner is the first player to make a line of 4 counters on their grid. The line can be along a row or a column or a diagonal.

Game: Dividing by 8

- Before you start, decide who is Player 1 and who is Player 2.
- Take turns to:
  - roll the dice
  - find a number on your grid that, when divided by 8, gives an answer that is either the two dice numbers or the sum of the two dice numbers
  - place a counter on that number.
- The winner is the first player to make a line of 4 counters on their grid. The line can be along a row or a column or a diagonal.

Q3 Multiply each number by 8.

3	7	5	10	4

Divide each number by 8.

48	72	8	16	64

Point to one of the numbers on the grids in the games, e.g. 24, and ask your child to divide this number by 8, i.e. 'What is 24 divided by 8?'.

Q1 Answer these.

$5 × 9 =$ ☐

$90 ÷ 9 =$ ☐

$72 ÷ 9 =$ ☐

$4 × 9 =$ ☐

$45 ÷ 9 =$ ☐

$7 × 9 =$ ☐

$27 ÷ 9 =$ ☐

$6 × 9 =$ ☐

$8 × 9 =$ ☐

$36 ÷ 9 =$ ☐

$3 × 9 =$ ☐

$90 ÷ 9 =$ ☐

$9 × 9 =$ ☐

$63 ÷ 9 =$ ☐

$54 ÷ 9 =$ ☐

$10 × 9 =$ ☐

$81 ÷ 9 =$ ☐

$2 × 9 =$ ☐

Q2 Write the missing numbers.

☐ $x 9 = 54$

☐ $÷ 9 = 9$

☐ $÷ 9 = 8$

☐ $x 9 = 27$

☐ $÷ 9 = 2$

☐ $÷ 9 = 6$

☐ $÷ 9 = 3$

☐ $x 9 = 18$

$10 x$ ☐ $= 90$

☐ $÷ 9 = 4$

☐ $x 9 = 45$

$72 ÷$ ☐ $= 9$

$9 x$ ☐ $= 36$

☐ $x 9 = 63$

☐ $÷ 9 = 5$

☐ $x 9 = 81$

☐ $÷ 9 = 7$

☐ $x 9 = 72$

Game: Multiplying and dividing by 9

Game: Multiplying by 9

You need: pencil, paper and playing cards with the Jacks, Queens and Kings removed

- Before you start:
  - shuffle the cards and place them face down in a pile
  - Decide who is Player 1 and who is Player 2.
- Take turns to:
  - turn over the top card
  - multiply the card number by 9
  - write down the answer.
- After 8 rounds, each player adds their 8 scores (you can use a calculator).
- The winner is the player with the larger total.

Round	Player 1	Player 2
1		
2		
3		
4		
5		
6		
7		
8		

Game: Dividing by 9

You need: counters and playing cards with the Jacks, Queens and Kings removed

- Shuffle the cards and place them face down in a pile.
- Take turns to:
  - turn over the top card
  - place a counter on a square whose calculation gives the answer on the card.
- The winner is the first player to complete a line of 3 counters. The line can be along a row or a column or a diagonal.

$18 \div 9$	$54 \div 9$	$45 \div 9$	$27 \div 9$
$45 \div 9$	$9 \div 9$	$36 \div 9$	$63 \div 9$
$9 \div 9$	$90 \div 9$	$72 \div 9$	$18 \div 9$
$81 \div 9$	$27 \div 9$	$36 \div 9$	$81 \div 9$
$72 \div 9$	$63 \div 9$	$90 \div 9$	$54 \div 9$

Q3 Complete the grids.

5	8	2
4	9	6
7	3	10

$\times 9 =$

45		
		27

18	45	63
36	90	54
72	81	27

$\div 9 =$

	5	
		3

Point to some division calculations on the grid in the Dividing by 9 game and ask your child to say the answers. Encourage your child to give quick responses to each question.

Q1 Complete the table.

×	7	2	10	1	6	4	8	3	9	5
3										
9			90							
4							32			
10										
6										
2										
8										
5										
7										

Q2 Divide each red number by 2 , 4 and 8.

Divide each blue number by 5 and 10.

Divide each green number by 3 , 6 and 9.

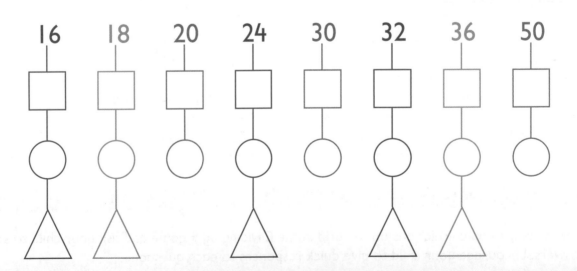

16   18   20   24   30   32   36   50

Game: Multiplication cards

- Before you start:
  - take 10 counters each
  - shuffle the cards and place them face down in a pile in the middle of the table.

- Take turns to turn over the top two cards, multiply the two numbers together and say the answer.

- The winner of the round is the player with the larger answer. The winner takes one of the other player's counters.

- Continue to pick up two cards each, and multiply the two numbers together.

- When all the cards have been used, the winner is the player with more counters.

You need: playing cards with the Jacks, Queens and Kings removed and 20 counters

4 times 8 equals 32

Q3

18	

means that you need to find two squares next to each other on the grid that multiply together to make 18.

Find these pairs of numbers on the grid.

18	

30	

56	

20	

63	

28	

30	

72	

50	

3	10	5	4
7	8	6	3
5	6	2	9
4	7	9	8

35	12	42	27	48

Say together the six times table forwards, then backwards. Then ask questions such as: 'What are three sixes? How many sixes in 42? What is six times four? What is fifty-four divided by six? Eight multiplied by six is...? Six times what equals sixty?' Repeat for other times tables.

Doubling is the same as **multiplying by 2**.

Example

Double 47 $(2 \times 40) + (2 \times 7)$
47 + 47   = 80 + 14
2×47 = 94

Q1 Double each of these numbers.

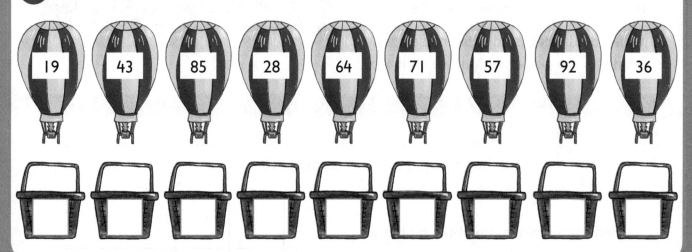

19   43   85   28   64   71   57   92   36

Q2 Double each of these numbers.

50   80   400   700

20   90   300   500

Halving is the same as **dividing by 2**.

Example

Halve 86   = (80 ÷ 2) + (6 ÷ 2)

86 ÷ 2   = 40 + 3

                = 43

Q3 Halve each of these numbers.

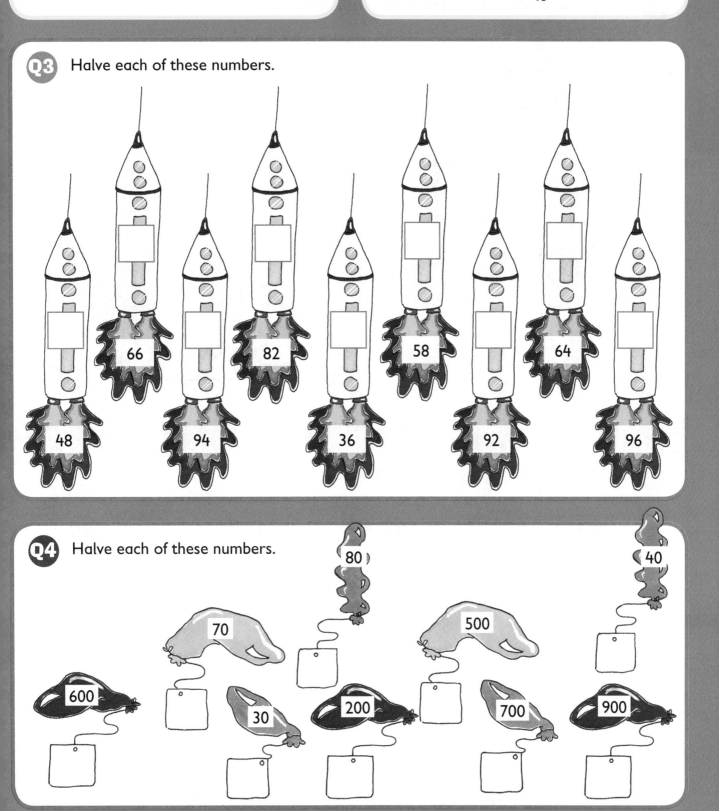

66   82   58   64

48   94   36   92   96

Q4 Halve each of these numbers.

80   40

70   500

600   30   200   700   900

Say any number less than 100, and ask your child to double the number. Use words such as: double, twice, two times. Repeat for the multiples of 10 and 100.

Q1 Write the numbers that come out of each machine.

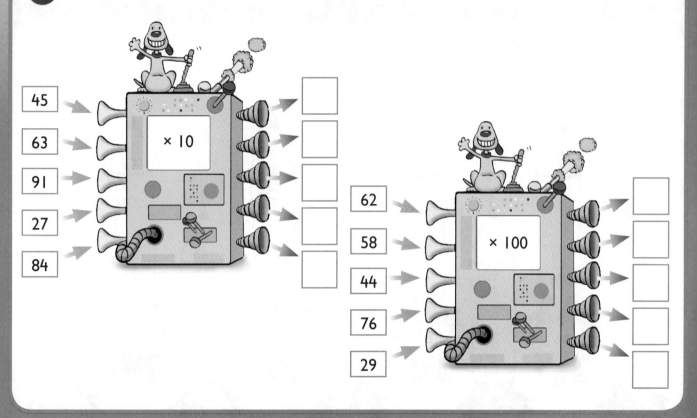

45
63
91
27
84

× 10

62
58
44
76
29

× 100

Q2 Multiply each number by 10 and 100.

× 10		× 100		× 10		× 100
	23				32	
	77				18	
	54				93	
	35				46	
	42				79	
	86				65	

Game: Multiplying by 10 and 100

- Before you start, shuffle the cards and place them face down in a pile in the middle of the table.
- Take turns to:
  - pick the top two cards from the pile and put each card on an empty box
  - do the calculations, and add the two answers together.
- The higher score wins and takes a counter.
- Play 5 rounds.

You need: pencil, paper, 5 counters and playing cards with the Jacks, Queens and Kings removed

× 10 =

× 100 =

Q3 Write the missing numbers

7 × ☐ = 700   27 × ☐ = 270   84 × ☐ = 8400

62 × ☐ = 620   18 × ☐ = 1800   95 × ☐ = 950

4 × ☐ = 40   81 × ☐ = 8100   50 × ☐ = 500

Look for 1-, 2- or 3-digit numbers, e.g. in newspapers, TV guides, on food packaging. Ask your child to multiply each number by 10 and 100. Encourage them to explain their thinking.

Q1 Write the numbers that come out of each machine.

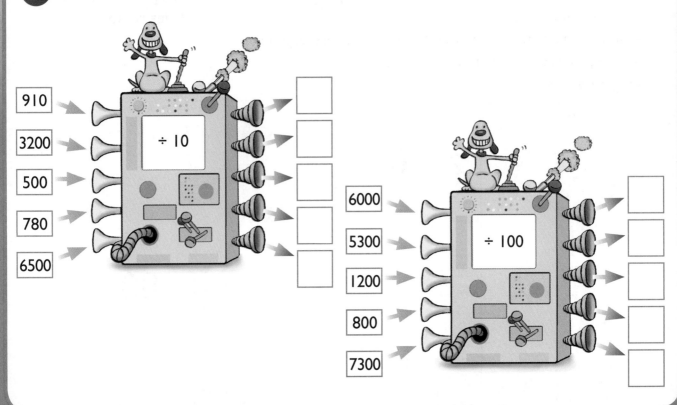

Q2 Divide each number by 10 and 100.

÷ 10		÷ 100	÷ 10		÷ 100
	300			8400	
	9400			5800	
	400			200	
	1600			4600	
	7500			900	
	2100			6200	

Game: Dividing by 10 and 100

- Before you start, shuffle the cards and place them face down in a pile in the middle of the table.
- Take turns to:
  – pick the top two cards from the pile and put each card on an empty box
  – do the calculations, and add the two answers together.
- The higher score wins and takes a counter.
- Play 5 rounds.

You need: pencil, paper, 5 counters and playing cards with the Jacks, Queens and Kings removed

$$00 \div 10 =$$

$$00 \div 100 =$$

 Q3 Write the missing numbers

$800 \div \boxed{} = 8$ $\qquad$ $510 \div \boxed{} = 51$ $\qquad$ $500 \div \boxed{} = 50$

$470 \div \boxed{} = 47$ $\qquad$ $9400 \div \boxed{} = 94$ $\qquad$ $8000 \div \boxed{} = 80$

$1200 \div \boxed{} = 12$ $\qquad$ $5600 \div \boxed{} = 560$ $\qquad$ $390 \div \boxed{} = 39$

Say different amounts of money (whole pounds only), e.g. £4, £17, £60, £120…. Ask your child to divide each amount by 10 and 100. Ask: 'How many pence in £4?' What is 400 pence divided by 10? What is 400 pence divided by 100?' Encourage them to explain their thinking.

When multiplying a 2-digit number by a 1-digit number,
we use both mental and written methods.

23×6

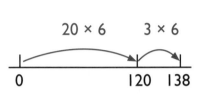

20 × 6   3 × 6

0   120   138

$$23 \times 6 = (20 \times 6) + (3 \times 6)$$
$$= 120 + 18$$
$$= 138$$

	20	3	
6	120	18	= 138

```
   23
 ×  6
  138
    1
```

Q1 For each of these multiplication calculations:
- estimate the answer
- work out the answer
- use a different method to check your answer.

		1st calculation	2nd calculation
76 x 8 = Estimate			
87 x 6 = Estimate			
96 x 7 = Estimate			

Q2 Arrange each set of digits to make a multiplication calculation, then work out the answer.

4
5
7

☐☐ × ☐ = ☐

3
8
6

☐☐ × ☐ = ☐

Q3 Multiply each blue number by a red number to give an answer that is a green number. Draw lines to link the red number to the blue number and the green number.

3	37	432
8	42	612
6	58	174
9	54	294
7	68	222

Q4 Use the digits 2 to 9 to complete each of these calculations. Each digit can only be used once.

| 2 | 3 | 4 | 5 | 6 | 7 | 8 | 9 |

$48 \times \boxed{} = 144$ $27 \times \boxed{} = 243$

$75 \times \boxed{} = 525$ $53 \times \boxed{} = 265$

$66 \times \boxed{} = 264$ $94 \times \boxed{} = 752$

$39 \times \boxed{} = 234$ $82 \times \boxed{} = 164$

Ask your child to write down a 2-digit number and a 1-digit number, e.g. 86 and 4. Then ask them to estimate the product of these two numbers. Ask: 'If you multiply 86 by 4, approximately what is the answer? How did you get that approximation? What digit will be in the units place? Why?'

When dividing a 2-digit number by a 1-digit number, we use both mental and written methods.

$93 \div 6$

$93 \div 6 = (60 + 33) \div 6$
$= 10 + 5 \text{ R } 3$
$= 15 \text{ R } 3$

	10	5 R 3	
6	60	33	$\rightarrow$

6	60	33

$$\begin{array}{r} 15 \text{ R } 3 \\ 6 \overline{)93} \\ \underline{60} \ (10 \times 6) \\ 33 \\ \underline{30} \ (5 \times 6) \\ 3 \end{array}$$

$$\begin{array}{r} 15 \text{ R } 3 \\ 6 \overline{)9^3 3} \end{array}$$

Q1 For each of these division calculations:
- estimate the answer
- work out the answer
- use a different method to check your answer.

	1st calculation	2nd calculation
$84 \div 6 =$ *Estimate* ( )		
$75 \div 4 =$ *Estimate* ( )		
$62 \div 3 =$ *Estimate* ( )		

Q2 Arrange each set of digits to make a division calculation, then work out the answer.

4
9
7

☐☐ ÷ ☐ = ☐

3
5
6

☐☐ ÷ ☐ = ☐

Q3 Divide each blue number by a red number to give an answer that is a green number. Draw lines to link the red number to the blue number and the green number.

64	3	14
98	6	18 R 2
56	7	12 R 4
79	5	14 R 1
85	4	19 R 3

Q4 Use the digits 2 to 9 to complete each of these calculations. Each digit can only be used once.

| 2 | 3 | 4 | 5 | 6 | 7 | 8 | 9 |

$55 \div \boxed{} = 13 \text{ R } 3$ $51 \div \boxed{} = 25 \text{ R } 1$

$96 \div \boxed{} = 10 \text{ R } 6$ $72 \div \boxed{} = 24$

$92 \div \boxed{} = 18 \text{ R } 2$ $95 \div \boxed{} = 13 \text{ R } 4$

$80 \div \boxed{} = 13 \text{ R } 2$ $91 \div \boxed{} = 11 \text{ R } 3$

Ask your child to write down a 2-digit number and a 1-digit number, e.g. 78 and 3. Ask: 'How would you work out what 78 divided by 3 is? Is there another way you could work it out?' Encourage your child to explain to you the different methods they could use to work out the answer.

Answers

2, 5 and 10 times tables

Page 4

1
$7 \times 2 = 14$	$9 \times 5 = 45$	$3 \times 10 = 30$
$5 \times 5 = 25$	$6 \times 10 = 60$	$10 \times 2 = 20$
$3 \times 5 = 15$	$9 \times 10 = 90$	$8 \times 2 = 16$

2
$5 \times 2 = 10$	$7 \times 5 = 35$	$6 \times 10 = 60$
$3 \times 2 = 6$	$2 \times 5 = 10$	$4 \times 10 = 40$
$2 \times 2 = 4$	$6 \times 5 = 30$	$8 \times 10 = 80$
$4 \times 2 = 8$	$3 \times 5 = 15$	$5 \times 10 = 50$
$8 \times 2 = 16$	$10 \times 5 = 50$	$9 \times 10 = 90$
$6 \times 2 = 12$	$5 \times 5 = 25$	$10 \times 10 = 100$
$10 \times 2 = 20$	$8 \times 5 = 40$	$7 \times 10 = 70$
$9 \times 2 = 18$	$4 \times 5 = 20$	$2 \times 10 = 20$

Page 5

3

×	5	2	8	6	1	10	4	9	7	3
2	10	4	16	12	2	20	8	18	14	6
5	25	10	40	30	5	50	20	45	35	15
10	50	20	80	60	10	100	40	90	70	30

Division facts related to the 2, 5 and 10 times tables

Page 6

1
$18 \div 2 = 9$	$40 \div 5 = 8$	$70 \div 10 = 7$
$20 \div 2 = 10$	$30 \div 5 = 6$	$25 \div 5 = 5$
$6 \div 2 = 3$	$40 \div 10 = 4$	$20 \div 10 = 2$

2
$10 \div 2 = 5$	$20 \div 5 = 4$	$30 \div 10 = 3$
$18 \div 2 = 9$	$45 \div 5 = 9$	$60 \div 10 = 6$
$16 \div 2 = 8$	$10 \div 5 = 2$	$80 \div 10 = 8$
$8 \div 2 = 4$	$30 \div 5 = 6$	$90 \div 10 = 9$
$14 \div 2 = 7$	$35 \div 5 = 7$	$70 \div 10 = 7$
$6 \div 2 = 3$	$40 \div 5 = 8$	$50 \div 10 = 5$
$12 \div 2 = 6$	$15 \div 5 = 3$	$100 \div 10 = 10$
$4 \div 2 = 2$	$50 \div 5 = 10$	$20 \div 10 = 2$

Page 7

3

Row 1: (45) 4 (⊗) (⊗) 12 8 (⊗) (⊗)
Row 2: (35) 2 (15) (⊗) 16 (⊗) (25)
Row 3: 14 (⊗) 5 6 (⊗) (⊗) 18 (⊗)

3 times table and the related division facts

Page 8

1
$2 \times 3 = 6$	$21 \div 3 = 7$	$6 \times 3 = 18$
$9 \div 3 = 3$	$8 \times 3 = 24$	$30 \div 3 = 10$
$6 \div 3 = 2$	$3 \times 3 = 9$	$12 \div 3 = 4$
$1 \times 3 = 3$	$27 \div 3 = 9$	$5 \times 3 = 15$
$24 \div 3 = 8$	$7 \times 3 = 21$	$3 \div 3 = 1$
$4 \times 3 = 12$	$9 \times 3 = 27$	$10 \times 3 = 30$

2
$5 \times 3 = 15$	$18 \div 3 = 6$
$4 \times 3 = 12$	$30 \div 3 = 10$
$1 \times 3 = 3$	$21 \div 3 = 7$
$3 \times 3 = 9$	$6 \div 3 = 2$
$8 \times 3 = 24$	$27 \div 3 = 9$

Page 9

3
$6 \times 3 = 18$	$6 \div 3 = 2$	$1 \times 3 = 3$
$21 \div 3 = 7$	$2 \times 3 = 6$	$15 \div 3 = 5$
$9 \times 3 = 27$	$12 \div 3 = 4$	$4 \times 3 = 12$
$8 \times 3 = 24$	$7 \times 3 = 21$	$9 \div 3 = 3$
$18 \div 3 = 6$	$27 \div 3 = 9$	$24 \div 3 = 8$

4 times table and the related division facts

Page 10

1
$5 \times 4 = 20$	$8 \div 4 = 2$	$7 \times 4 = 28$
$12 \div 4 = 3$	$8 \times 4 = 32$	$32 \div 4 = 8$
$20 \div 4 = 5$	$6 \times 4 = 24$	$16 \div 4 = 4$
$2 \times 4 = 8$	$40 \div 4 = 10$	$4 \times 4 = 16$
$36 \div 4 = 9$	$24 \div 4 = 6$	$28 \div 4 = 7$
$3 \times 4 = 12$	$10 \times 4 = 40$	$9 \times 4 = 36$

2 32 12 6 9 20 4

Page 11

3
$3 \times 4 = 12$	$16 \div 4 = 4$	$5 \times 4 = 20$
$32 \div 4 = 8$	$2 \times 4 = 8$	$9 \times 4 = 36$
$6 \times 4 = 24$	$8 \div 4 = 2$	$36 \div 4 = 9$
$24 \div 4 = 6$	$4 \times 4 = 16$	$8 \times 4 = 32$
$28 \div 4 = 7$	$7 \times 4 = 28$	$20 \div 4 = 5$

6 times table and the related division facts

Page 12

1
$7 \times 6 = 42$	$24 \div 6 = 4$	$5 \times 6 = 30$
$18 \div 6 = 3$	$9 \times 6 = 54$	$42 \div 6 = 7$
$36 \div 6 = 6$	$4 \times 6 = 24$	$54 \div 6 = 9$
$10 \times 6 = 60$	$12 \div 6 = 2$	$6 \times 6 = 36$
$30 \div 6 = 5$	$2 \times 6 = 12$	$48 \div 6 = 8$
$3 \times 6 = 18$	$60 \div 6 = 10$	$8 \times 6 = 48$

2
$2 \times 6 = 12$	$24 \div 6 = 4$	$6 \times 6 = 36$
$48 \div 6 = 8$	$3 \times 6 = 18$	$9 \times 6 = 54$
$60 \div 6 = 10$	$10 \times 6 = 60$	$18 \div 6 = 3$
$7 \times 6 = 42$	$12 \div 6 = 2$	$4 \times 6 = 24$
$36 \div 6 = 6$	$5 \times 6 = 30$	$30 \div 6 = 5$
$42 \div 6 = 7$	$54 \div 6 = 9$	$8 \times 6 = 48$

Page 13

3

Top boxes: 9 × 6 | 7 × 6 | 5 × 6 | 4 × 6 | 6 × 6

Number row: 42 3 18 16 32 24 40 54 6 20 26 30 52 48 56 12 65 60 36 10

Bottom boxes: 1 × 6 | 8 × 6 | 3 × 6 | 10 × 6 | 2 × 6

7 times table and the related division facts

Page 14

1
$3 \times 7 = 21$	$21 \div 7 = 3$	$5 \times 7 = 35$
$14 \div 7 = 2$	$4 \times 7 = 28$	$56 \div 7 = 8$
$35 \div 7 = 5$	$10 \times 7 = 70$	$63 \div 7 = 9$
$8 \times 7 = 56$	$49 \div 7 = 7$	$6 \times 7 = 42$
$28 \div 7 = 4$	$2 \times 7 = 14$	$70 \div 7 = 10$
$7 \times 7 = 49$	$42 \div 7 = 6$	$9 \times 7 = 63$

2 49 63 56 28 3 5 6 2

Page 15

3
$5 \times 7 = 35$	$14 \div 7 = 2$	$10 \times 7 = 70$
$49 \div 7 = 7$	$7 \times 7 = 49$	$28 \div 7 = 4$
$6 \times 7 = 42$	$63 \div 7 = 9$	$8 \times 7 = 56$
$21 \div 7 = 3$	$3 \times 7 = 21$	$35 \div 7 = 5$
$42 \div 7 = 6$	$56 \div 7 = 8$	$4 \times 7 = 28$

8 times table and the related division facts

Page 16

1
$3 \times 8 = 24$	$24 \div 8 = 3$	$9 \times 8 = 72$
$80 \div 8 = 10$	$6 \times 8 = 48$	$16 \div 8 = 2$
$64 \div 8 = 8$	$10 \times 8 = 80$	$72 \div 8 = 9$
$5 \times 8 = 40$	$32 \div 8 = 4$	$2 \times 8 = 16$
$40 \div 8 = 5$	$56 \div 8 = 7$	$48 \div 8 = 6$
$7 \times 8 = 56$	$8 \times 8 = 64$	$4 \times 8 = 32$

2
$6 \times 8 = 48$	$64 \div 8 = 8$	$8 \times 4 = 32$
$16 \div 8 = 2$	$3 \times 8 = 24$	$2 \times 8 = 16$
$80 \div 10 = 8$	$9 \times 8 = 72$	$56 \div 8 = 7$
$8 \times 8 = 64$	$24 \div 8 = 3$	$7 \times 8 = 56$
$40 \div 8 = 5$	$5 \times 8 = 40$	$48 \div 8 = 6$
$72 \div 8 = 9$	$32 \div 8 = 4$	$10 \times 8 = 80$

Page 17

3

3	7	5	10	4
24	56	40	80	32

48	72	8	16	64
6	9	1	2	8

9 times table and the related division facts

Page 18

1
$5 \times 9 = 45$	$27 \div 9 = 3$	$9 \times 9 = 81$
$90 \div 9 = 10$	$6 \times 9 = 54$	$63 \div 9 = 7$
$72 \div 9 = 8$	$8 \times 9 = 72$	$54 \div 9 = 6$
$4 \times 9 = 36$	$36 \div 9 = 4$	$10 \times 9 = 90$
$45 \div 9 = 5$	$3 \times 9 = 27$	$81 \div 9 = 9$
$7 \times 9 = 63$	$90 \div 9 = 10$	$2 \times 9 = 18$